MW00917248

The Official Teen Survival Guide For Getting Over A Breakup

22 STEPS You Can Take RIGHT NOW to Begin Healing

Emilee Day

Copyright © 2015 Emilee Day

All Rights Reserved. This Book or any portion thereof may
not be reproduced or used in any manner

Table of Contents

"I gave him a piece of my heart a long time ago, and once you give that away, I've learned you don't so easily get it back."

– Laura Miller, For All You Have Left

Emilee's Introduction

*E*very book has a story within a story.

In this case, it is your love story.

It is about your unique experience, your dizzying heights of first love and your fall to the depths of anguish following the break-up.

You will live your own experience through the pages, just as I will use mine for the inspiration to write it.

This is your book about finding love, experiencing it for the wondrous thing it is, and then losing it and trying to live with the emptiness that is left.

It is about young love that feels as if our generation invented it. It's about instant connection, rapid-fire courtships, passion, and the all-encompassing, soul-kindling, body-heating, brain takeover kind of love that requires all your energy to sustain.

As we start, I will share my story so that you may feel free to share yours.

Dylan (his name has been changed to protect the guilty) and I met in Grade 11 and by the summer before we entered our graduate year, we were everything to each other. We couldn't bear to be parted; our lives were completely entwined and we were planning to have a perfect life together.

I wanted to study psychology at a university upstate, but he wanted to take engineering in our hometown so he could live with his parents and save money for our pending marriage when we got our degrees.

If he could make such a sacrifice for our future, so could I. I went to study at the same university he was attending and by making a lot of adjustments, I could work on a Bachelor of Arts with a lot of psychology courses. It was close enough to the career I wanted.

I've read about idyllic love in Jane Austin novels but couldn't imagine ever using the word myself, but I started to write it now in my diary. He was roguishly handsome with those deep blue teasing eyes that could see right through me. He completed me; he was charming and outgoing and a perfect balance to my shyness. Together we could do anything.

We both had part-time jobs to help with tuition, so spending as much time together as we wanted was a little difficult. But when we were together, the sparks still ignited and I felt like I was the luckiest person in the world.

I worked at a coffee shop and he worked in a small shipping facility on the edge of town. One night when he was working and I was able to get off early, I decided to do something really romantic. I knew he had a break around 9:30 p.m. on his shift that went to midnight, so I packed a great little picnic with his favorite sandwiches and decided to surprise him.

There was nobody in the front part of the warehouse when I walked in, but when he was filing the day's paperwork, he was often in a little office at the back so I went in quietly to surprise him.

I didn't even have to open the door to hear the voices. And through the office window I could see that he had my best friend Sarah (name changed) on the desk and was having his own kind of picnic.

I shrunk into the darkness rather than confront them. Silly, I know, but I was just numb. For three more weeks, I actually didn't say anything, hoping that it would all just go away. I ate ice cream by the tub and I still lost weight. I couldn't focus on my schoolwork. I didn't even want to leave my room.

I asked him once if we were still good and he said of course we were. And then, sort of out of the blue, he sent me a text saying it was hard to tell me in person and it had nothing to do with me and everything to do with him, but he wanted to see other people.

I honestly don't know to this day which action made me the angriest, the fact that he cheated on me or that he dumped me with a text. A text! He didn't even have the courage to look me in the eye and dare to say he was leaving to my face. I was absolutely livid! That lying, cheating, two-timing jerk thought he could get me out of his life with a text!

I'd like to say I summoned my dignity and just stalked out of his life. I'd like to say it, but it wouldn't be true. This was the man I planned to marry and have babies with! I needed to talk it out with him, or at least let him know of my anger.

I made mistake number one. I called him. I made him listen to all the hurt, the pain, the anger and the tally of his totally despicable actions. I screamed a lot and he deserved to hear it.

I told him I knew he was already seeing someone else and that I'd known it for some time and asked how he could screw my best friend. Then I screamed more, which was really more satisfying than any answer he offered.

He stayed calm and just said he still wanted to be friends and he felt we were just moving too fast. He said what I saw didn't really mean anything, that he just wanted to see what it was like to be with someone else.

Looking back at the journals I kept in the weeks that followed, I could say now that the bones of this book were created then.

First love. First loss.

I know there are horrible forms of torture in this world, but for you and me, can any pain be worse than the one you endure when your first love ends?

It puts your brain and your heart and your soul in a vice and slowly and steadily tightens it until you feel like all of the life is being squeezed out of you.

The short version of my story is that I did recover after a lot of trial and error, and I went on to get a graduate degree in psychology. One of my key areas of research was in relationships and love and what I studied, coupled with my own experience, prepared me to write this book that I hope will help you.

I have recovered. I have learned again to see value in myself and to understand that I deserve a better relationship than the one I had. I deserve not to be cheated on.

When many months later I got to the point where I could think of my first love again without fury or tears, I knew I was healing.

The next step of my recovery process was learning that had Dylan not ended the relationship when he did, in the next year or so, I would likely have initiated the split. Looking back, I can see that we were growing farther apart as we were growing up.

I had more dreams and more ambitions and I could never have settled within the dimensions that he found comfortable.

In other words, I learned a lot from what happened, and as painful as the process was, it wasn't all bad. The happiness I am capable of experiencing today in a relationship could never have developed without that first love.

As I take you through the healing process, chapter by chapter, I hope that you too can learn more about yourself as you recover.

I work a lot with teens and adolescents and people in their early 20s who are experiencing the downside of their ending their relationships. I am able to counsel them through their break-ups and help them work their way back to a state of normal for them, but it is never easy.

Just as there are identifiable sources of grief when a loved one dies, there is a process to coping with their disengagement from your life. You feel devalued when you are dumped, and unworthy because you have been rejected. You feel like you failed to be enough of a person, and you wonder if you will ever find love again.

I have compiled techniques for recovery from relationships that work, and I will share all of them in this book. It is now the ultimate survival guide to getting over your break-up.

When you read this book you will learn:

- Why you will never completely get over your break-up and why that's okay

- How one bittersweet experience must be handled right so it does not hurt your ability to love fully again

- How to handle a bad break-up and keep your health and dignity intact

- How to handle the emotional roller coaster of the post break-up days

- What to do and what not to do when a relationship goes bad

- How to use your vulnerability to get in touch with negative feelings and destroy them

- How to rebuild your life and learn to love yourself as well as others

There is no one-size-fits-all guide to healing a broken heart, but there are many common traits that link those who recover. That is the focus of this book which I hope will help you through these tough times.

From Taylor Swift to Ariana Grande to Justin Bieber, even the rich and famous have endured heartbreak when their first relationships broke up. You will recover.

However, if at any point in your post break-up days you feel so desperate that you don't think you can go on, please seek professional help immediately. Everyone has different degrees of tolerance to emotional pain. Find the level of help you need.

CHAPTER 1

HOW SOCIETY SETS US UP TO BELIEVE OUR FIRST LOVE WILL LAST

I maybe had a first love and had my heart broken, but reflecting on it, I don't think that was love. I think as I'm getting older and having more in-depth relationships, maybe I'll experience it. At the moment, I don't know, exactly, if I've been in love.

– Selena Gomez

You were just coming out of math class and rushing across your sprawling high school to the English wing when you rounded a corner and walked right into him.

He touched both your arms just above the elbows to steady you gently and a feeling like you had never experienced overwhelmed you.

His eyes were gentle, laughing, and he said, "Whoa there. It's not a race," and you laughed. He helped you pick up your books and asked where you were going in such a hurry.

Suddenly, you were no longer in a hurry. All you wanted to do was prolong this conversation.

Within a few minutes you fell madly in love with him, and soon you were dating and he was officially your guy.

The first time he kissed you the world did literally skip an orbit. You may forget a lot of the kisses you get in your life, but you will never forget that one. Ever.

When you are a teenager or young adult in love for the first time, just what exactly is it that you fall into?

"Fallen" is a good word, because in fact the experience of being in love is an experience different from anything in your world previously. You are emotionally taken to the edge of a cliff and you slide off into a place that is so complex and compelling that you jump even without knowing if you have any place to land.

There is no feeling like it, and that is why stories about first love have filled thousands of book pages for over hundreds of years. It is the fodder of diaries and journals and a fire that burns forever with you, even into old age.

You grew up knowing that someday it would happen. After all, since you were little you saw that society supported the idea that we would all find our perfect partner. Ken had Barbie. Rapunzel had her prince. But it still catches you unaware.

You will love many people in your life, but you will never love anyone quite as passionately as you love the first person who defines true love for you.

Your first love is all-consuming. It becomes more important than anything else that is happening in your world. Before you met the boy or girl of your dreams, your rational mind was focused on your academic work, your after-school job, your pending holiday with your parents, and what you and your friends were going to do on Saturday night.

Suddenly, all you really want is to spend time with your special love. You can't talk to them enough; they enter your thoughts last thing at night and first thing in the morning. You start to plan your life around your availability to be with them.

You are each the primary person on the other's mind in those first golden moments. You want to spend every moment exploring this compelling relationship to the point that you are willing to sacrifice other important relationships like close friends, siblings and parents.

In the depth of this kind of passion and absorption, you look at other relationships and consider them shallow compared to the depth of feeling you have for your beloved.

You are super sensitive to each other, picking up the merest glimmer of an eye, arch of a brow, secretive smile and brush of bodies against each other, even in a public place.

With the same intuitiveness, both of you are hurt by the smallest slight.

When parents or friends caution against this new love that is dominating your life and causing you to compromise other things they think are important, you react resentfully and resolve to double your intent to dedicate yourself to the relationship.

In your eyes, you have found the person you want to be with for the rest of your life. You cannot contemplate time away from this passion of yours. You may experiment for the first time with sexual intimacy to gratify your intense emotional connection.

You believe that nothing will ever be better in this world than the way that you feel right now. In truth, perhaps it never will.

The trouble is, that in the vast majority of cases, this euphoric love just will not last.

In the next chapter, we will explore what happens and why it's so hard to deal with a breakup.

CHAPTER 2

BREAKING UP IS VERY HARD TO DO

"Maybe not," she said as we came to the car. "But maybe that isn't so bad. You can't love anyone that way more than once in a lifetime. It's too hard and it hurts too much when it ends. The first boy is always the hardest to get over, Haven. It's just the way the world works."

– Sarah Dessen, That Summer

*I*f you are between the ages of 15 and 25 and experiencing your first love affair, statistically you are a broken heart just waiting to happen.

Logically, there is a good reason for this. No matter how close you are, you will likely grow apart because you got together before either one of you really knew your own selves. Youth is a time of self-discovery, and the first relationships are often just part of that process, even though it masquerades as something much more intense.

Dr. Andra Brosh, an authority on youthful love affairs and co-founder of Divorce Detox, said in a blog post with Kourney Jason ("Surviving A Divorce in Your 20s: What You Should Now" published Jan. 31, 2012) that our brains are not even fully developed until we are 25, so managing a serious and committed relationship will inevitably become a problem.

What you feel is real at the time you are experiencing it. But what you will feel as you find yourself in a broader world is not real to you yet, and that colors what happens next.

Brosh also says that most teens and adolescents haven't been able to develop the necessary skills to sustain a healthy relationship. These things include expertise in good communication techniques, problem solving skills, and personal responsibility.

If you live in the public eye like celebrities, your youthful first loves are fodder for the tabloids and there is no hiding your tears if a break-up occurs. Think of Avril Lavigne, married at 21 to Deryck Whibley and divorced three years later, a 23-year-old Scarlett Johansson marrying Ryan Reynolds and divorcing him three years later, and Britney Spears, married and divorced twice by the time she was 24.

When your first love is in your teen years, it is rare that it will survive. One of you will fall out of love with the other, leading to the inevitable heartbreak that is quite possibly the worst pain you will endure for the rest of your life.

Often times the relationship falls on hard times when you have to separate after graduation to pursue different career paths and schools or seize opportunities for adventure in the big world that is opening up before you. And as beautiful as falling in love is, falling out of love is desperately painful.

If you are the one who has been betrayed or dumped, you will feel abandoned, rejected, helpless, angry and hurt.

You may want to express your hurt and anger to your former love, or you may turn your hurt and anger on yourself. Either way, it is extremely difficult to overcome what is happening to you emotionally.

In the most extreme of situations, you feel that you cannot live without your lover. If you have that thought, run, don't walk, to your guidance counselor, the school psychologist, parent or trusted adult and tell them you need help.

In truth, in the long run, whether you or your partner initiated the break-up doesn't matter. The reality you must face is that yesterday you were in an exhilarating couple relationship and today you are walking alone.

You sense that you have failed somehow and you do not believe in that moment that you will ever love again. Well-meaning friends and parents give you the old "more fish in the sea than that one" story, but you don't want to talk about other fish. You want to talk about your love and the fact that they are gone and you cannot bear it.

Interestingly enough, even if you were the one who initiated the break-up, there are times when you will still feel bad. You feel ashamed, sad, and as if you have broken a commitment and you did not really want to hurt somebody. You just wanted your freedom to move on and see other people.

Lots of things change in life, but nothing is as difficult to adjust to as the changes of relationships. Your relationship changes not only with the person you broke up with, but also with your friends (who may still want to be friends with both of you) and with your daily routine.

Even simple questions like what to do the next weekend are a whole new area that must be considered.

Why are our first loves so hard to get over?

In an article called "Heartbreak and Home Runs: The Power of First Experience" (written by Jay Dixit and published Jan. 1, 2010 on the Psychology Today website), Northwestern University psychologist Dan McAdams says part of the problem is the way your brain remembers things.

McAdams, author of *The Redemptive Self: Stories Americans Live By*, notes that a lot of the pain comes down to our autobiographical memories, the stories of how we see our lives in terms of who we are, who we were and who we might be in the future.

If you look at the stories of your life when you are older, a big chapter near the front of the book will focus on your first love, just as other chapters will deal with your first job, your first child and even your first big trip.

"'Firsts' impact us powerfully because they are remembered autobiographically with a clarity that never fades like other memories do," McAdams suggests.

"Noting that, you may not remember the fourth real kiss you had, or the twentieth, but you will always remember the first." He says this is natural and is referred to as the primacy effect.

David Pillemer, a psychologist from the University of New Hampshire, concurs. The author of *Momentous Event, Vivid Memories,* he has done a lot of research into how and what we remember of the events of our lives.

He discovered that when psychologists questioned seniors about the main events of their lives, the ones they most often recall are the things that happened to them in their late teens and early 20s.

Known as the early memory bump, these memories come back to us the most because that is the time period when we experience the most firsts in our lives, including our first love.

One psychologist actually specializes in studying first kisses: John Bohannon III at Butler University. He describes the first kiss as a feeling of heightened reality or unreality. It is so powerful we feel disembodied from the world.

Another reason we have so much trouble getting over our first loves is because it creates something in our memory that psychologists call "flashbulb memories." Because it engages all our senses simultaneously, as do experiences like our first day of school, the birth of a first child or even our first view of the ocean or a mountain range, it is embedded in our brain forever.

You know now that you are never going to forget your first love, but what else makes it unique from any other relationship you are going to have in your life?

It is the first and only time you will fall in love without ever having had your heart broken before. You have no guard up. You don't know when that person is getting too close or the relationship is getting too all-encompassing. You don't even recognize the signs when he or she starts behaving in a way that would signal a pending break-up to someone more experienced in love and life.

You live in love totally in the moment. There is no past to compare it to and the future is just a dream you believe will go on forever.

The downside of that is when the break-up happens; you also have no compass to show you the way out of the horrible pain and rejection you feel.

All changes in life involve stress, but nothing can compare to the loss of your first love.

If you do not handle it healthily, it could hamper your ability to have good relationships for the rest of your life. It can make you unable to trust again or to feel safe and loved in a relationship. You may find it hard to commit or accept a commitment in the future if you cannot come to terms with what has happened.

Susan Andersen, a psychologist at New York University, says that first relationships can create a template that will get activated each time you begin to fall in love. Even if you meet a person who reminds you of your former love, it will trigger the template you have in your memory.

This template effect is known as transference. You don't just see the new person as someone who reminds you of your ex-love, you see them as someone you immediately want to be close to and begin the behavior you engaged in with your ex.

Loving and losing is a complicated experience in life. There is certainly no one-size-fits-all way to come out of your break-ups well, but there are a lot of innovative thoughts and actions you can take to adapt to what has happened and live comfortably with its memory.

In the chapters that follow, we will present these ideas to you as a guide to getting over those who have broken your heart.

CHAPTER 3

MAKING SENSE OF YOUR BROKEN RELATIONSHIP

"Love hurts. First love is excruciating. Like being burned in orange flames and then cast into icy water. Your emotions change from one second to the next. You can't sleep. You never sleep. First love is a form of dying and being reborn."

– Chloe Thurlow, Snow Falls Softly

You know now that good love can go bad. You know that even when you love someone with all your heart, you can lose them.

We are going to introduce you to some of the best coping strategies available gathered from professionals and the people like you who have experienced a break-up and found their own creative ways to deal with their emotions when that happens.

What makes this book unique is that we are concerned only with you and your emotions as you work through the trauma of getting over some your first relationships.

We need to give you the means to create your own personal strategy to get back to living a full life.

The first thing to understand is that no matter how strong you think you are, you are going to experience a lot of different emotions as you go through your break-up.

Just as there are stages of grief when someone close to you dies, there are stages of enduring a break-up. Some teens have said it is almost harder to recover from a break-up than a death, because not only must you mourn the loss of love, but you must learn to see your ex-love happy with someone else. You cannot just run and hide. Your paths will cross over and over again, and each time you feel like you will die again emotionally.

You have to find ways to deal with the fear of being alone again and the insecurity of thinking that because one love left you, others may do the same. You believe in that moment that you will never have true love again, and the anger, the hurt, the sense of failure, the sadness, the defiance and the loneliness overwhelm you.

How you handle the days and weeks following a break-up will impact the rest of your life.

The rational part of you reminds you that you must go on.

But how do you find strength when you are so vulnerable? How do you ever think happy thoughts again when you are now consumed with darkness? How do you even get out of bed and walk back into your school or your workplace? And what happens the first time you encounter your ex after your break-up?

Our process for total recovery is built on one premise.

No matter how horrible you feel, you will get better if you just do one little thing every day towards your long-term survival.

Just one thing.

You don't have to do it all at once. You don't need to make huge life decisions or stop crying or immediately "get over it" as friends will advise you.

You just need to do one constructive little thing every day and you will come back stronger, happier and more capable of getting and giving love than you could ever imagine.

We will show you how.

Before we get into the specifics, here's one thought that will help. It comes from the work of Byron Katie, a woman who was once so depressed that she couldn't leave her bedroom.

One day she realized that the world she thought was outside her bedroom walls was a projection of her mind, not reality. It was too frightening for her to face only because she thought it was.

She wrote a landmark book about accepting change in our lives called *Loving What Is. I Need Your Love - Is That True?* In it she introduced the world to "The Work," a process millions of people have used since that time to find comfort in times of intense pain and grief.

It is now discussed throughout the world at free public events as people with genuine hurt and sorrow in their hearts gather to mourn and end up questioning their own idea of reality.

Before we go into the day-to-day actions you can take to overcome a bad break-up, we want to introduce you to the idea of The Work because it may be the fastest, best way to start the process of recovery for you. It certainly worked for me.

Byron Katie told the world something we had never really considered before. She said that all our thoughts are harmless and can't hurt us until we believe them.

"It's not our thoughts, but the attachments to our thoughts, that causes suffering," she wrote.

If we want to recover from anything horrible that has happened to us in life, especially a bad break-up, we need to address our thoughts, even our fearful, awful ones, and accept them openly without judging ourselves. There is no point in denying the thoughts that torment us when we are lovesick. Rather, we need to consider the thoughts and why we are having them and accept that it is okay to have them.

When you accept that it is okay to think what you think, regardless of how black and negative and depressing it is, then you can start to heal by taking your thoughts, one by one, and putting them through The Work.

For each thought you have, ask yourself these four questions:

1. Is it true?

2. Can you absolutely know it's true?

3. How do you react when you believe that thought?

4. Who would you be without that thought?

It is an incredible way to see what you really think about your ex-boyfriend or ex-girlfriend. Eventually, when you take every thought you have about them and put it through those four questions, you start to understand that everything outside of you is a reflection of how you think inside.

In the case of a break-up, common thoughts that will fill your brain are that the other person never really loved you, that they set out deliberately to hurt you, that they are horrible and mean people, and that the break-up should never have happened.

In other words, the thoughts you have conflict with the reality of what has happened. Like it or not your love has left, and whether the break-up should have happened or not, it has and it is a real factor in your life that you must now deal with.

In the case of your break-up, let's start with the first most common thought, which is that the other person never really loved you.

Do you know if that thought is true? Not really. For a while, it seemed as if they really did care for you a great deal. Was it all an illusion? You don't know if that is true.

Can you absolutely know that they didn't love you, even at the beginning of the relationship? No, you cannot absolutely say that. You could not get in your partner's head and know for sure their motivation from the start.

How do you react when you believe that thought to be true?

You are absolutely devastated. You feel the deepest possible betrayal. You feel ashamed and even embarrassed that you let yourself love as much as you did. You feel worthless. You feel lower than low.

Who would you be without that thought?

You would feel a little bit better. At least you would know that there was love at the start, and that would set up a foundation for healing after the break-up. You could start to understand that in truth, perhaps the two of you had been growing apart. You would not feel worthless. You would know that you had the power to attract this person and to have them fall in love with you, if only for a little while.

Taking this one thought through The Work can start your process of healing. You start to understand that perhaps through your thoughts you can have some degree of control on whether you are okay or devastated. If you can keep trying to sort out your imagined thoughts from reality, perhaps you can heal just a little bit each day.

What else can you do to recover? In the coming chapters, we will give you twenty more ways to rebuild your life after your break-up and emerge stronger, more loving and more confident than you could ever imagine.

CHAPTER 4

HOW TO LEARN TO BE KIND TO YOURSELF

"We spend so much of our passion on our first love. I'm not convinced that it – passion – is one of those things that you have an endless amount of – like happiness and sadness. I could be happy all day. I could be sad all day. But I'm not so sure I'll ever love like that again."

– Laura Miller

*I*f you fall hard onto a cement surface and break your ribs, nobody can heal them for you. They hurt when you cough, when you laugh, when you get up and when you sit down. They hurt when somebody tries to hug you and they hurt when you push somebody away.

The doctor can give you a pain killer to get you through the first tough days, but then you are on your own and still in pain. Your friends and family can sympathize with you and show you extra care and attention, but ultimately they get wrapped up in their own worlds again and you are on your own, still hurting. People give you advice that doesn't work and tell you that time will heal the broken ribs, but you aren't even listening. What they suggest doesn't work and you don't want to wait for time to heal the break; you want the pain to be gone right now.

A broken heart is a lot like that. Those who care about you shower you with attention and well-meaning advice. None of it works, either because it's not relevant to how you feel, they just don't understand what really happened, or they can't relate to your unique circumstances and responses.

After a while they refocus on other things, and you are still alone and you still hurt.

This is the time when you most need to learn to be kind to yourself.

This is when you have to start taking one small step toward recovery each day.

In this chapter and those that follow, we will outline these steps. You don't have to take them in sequence, but you can and they will help. But as long as you do something to heal each day, you will grow strong again.

RECOVERY PRACTICE # 1 – YOU NEED TLC SO TAKE IT NOW

Practice number one on the road to recovery after your break-up is to practice kindness on yourself. Understand that only you can heal your hurt and it will take as much time as it takes. There is no formula to compute to tell you when your heart will stop aching and your thoughts will brighten. It will happen when it is ready and nobody, including you, can predict when that will be.

So just as with healing broken ribs, move slowly and tentatively in the beginning. Take a baby step here, a baby step there. Praise yourself when you accomplish one step after another and try to focus less and less on your pain.

No one can say how long it will take, but know for sure that healing will begin the minute you ask for it to begin.

Understand that when others bombard you with advice they aren't trying to upset you; rather, they do mean well. You can accept their invitations and start to go out again, or you can rest from the comfort of your bedroom; it doesn't matter. Only you know how you can function.

Think of ways you can treat yourself. It may be as simple as a shoe-shopping excursion or a pedicure at the local spa. Or you might surrender to a night of ice cream and potato chips (just one night) or watch old movies from your bed. It might be allowing yourself to get immersed in a book for an hour and letting it totally take over your thoughts, crowding out the pain.

It doesn't matter what your indulgence is, just make it happen and accept it happily for all it is worth. You've been through a lot and you need a little tender loving care. Who better to know just what is needed than you?

RECOVERY PRACTICE # 2 – IT'S YOUR BREAK-UP SO CRY IF YOU WANT TO

A good cry can be effective when you are so sad you don't know what to do. We are raised to consider crying a weakness, but the latest research contradicts that. Crying can be useful in launching the emotional healing process.

Dr. Jerry Bergman, in an article called "The Miracle of Tears" published in *Creation*, Vol. 15, No. 4, Sept. 1993, says that tears work so well that we tend to take them for granted. Besides the physical things they do for us like clear out our eyes, kill bacteria and remove toxins, they can elevate our mood.

When you cry, your manganese level is lowered. That's a good thing, because manganese is linked to nervousness, irritability, and emotional disturbance. In essence, you can cry yourself happy.

Crying also removes some chemicals that cause stress in your body such as the endorphins leucine-enkaphalin and prolactin, which affects your overall mood and stress tolerance.

If you really, really want to cry but you feel you can't or that it is inappropriate, you are just making things worse. Holding back your tears will weaken you, rather than making you stronger. It will increase your stress levels and contribute to diseases aggravated by stress like ulcers, heart problems and high blood pressure.

Even if you cry in front of strangers, you will be amazed at the kindness and gentleness of people who offer assistance.

You can justify the tears if you need to. You have not just lost the one you love, but also the many parts of your life that were folded into that relationship. You lost your day-to-day and weekend routine, you lost regular companionship and sex, you lost your primary emotional supporter, and you lost some dreams and hopes for life in the future.

That is a lot to be lost and grief is inevitable. You can store it all up inside of you and just wait for the stress dam to burst, or you can let the tears spill over, as often and for as long as you want, and drain that emotional reservoir until, spent and exhausted, you realize you have no tears left. At the end of the crying stage comes a new beginning.

RECOVERY PRACTICE # 3 – TAKE THE HELPING HANDS THAT ARE EXTENDED

When it comes to recovering from a bad break-up, self-reliance is greatly over-rated. What you need more than that is to look up and see a circle of helping hands, all extended, all full of a different kind of love, all reaching to pull you back onto your feet.

This is not the time to push everyone away; it is the time to allow yourself to accept the hands that are offered to you.

There is a danger that walks hand-in-hand with loss, and that is the danger of developing depression. If your sadness is absolutely overwhelming and fills your heart day in and day out to the point that you cannot even get out of bed or get dressed to greet the day, take the next hand that comes your way and tell them you need help to get over this trauma.

There are professional counselors in every community who are trained and capable of helping you. It is a rare person who gets all the way through life without turning to them at some point. If this is your point, get an appointment, get dressed and get going.

You don't have to do everything on your own.

Sometimes when we are going through a break-up we even shut ourselves off from our friends and parents who want to help. We mistakenly think that heartache is our burden to bear alone.

It's not, and there isn't a person on this planet that doesn't get their heart broken sooner or later. If your friends haven't experienced it yet, they can learn from you. If they have, they can give you sympathy and company, and assist you greatly in the healing process.

Your friends will generally fall into two groups: the ones who want to mourn with you and the ones who to make you happy again. You need both approaches.

People want to help. Let them. That is another kind of love and a sustaining one. Don't shut yourself off from it.

CHAPTER 5

DEALING WITH THE ONE WHO BROKE YOUR HEART: DOS AND DON'TS

"Did I think he was 'the one'? I'll never know. At sixteen, everyone is 'the one'."

– K.A. Tucker, Ten Tiny Breaths

Most of us get into relationships with people in our schools, in our communities or in our workplaces. When the break-up happens, one of the toughest things is that you will encounter them again and again, and you have to be able to do that successfully without breaking down or causing a scene. This chapter's tips for getting over your break-up focus on how to handle your ex.

RECOVERY PRACTICE # 4 – DON'T HOOK UP WITH YOUR EX. WE MEAN IT.

Once the break-up occurs, your feelings for your ex don't just evaporate. Your love may be tinged with hate, anger, grief and even thoughts of revenge, but there will be strong feelings for quite some time as you work it all through.

For that reason, the absolute best course of action is to cut off communication with your ex as quickly as possible. If they keep trying to call you, text you or encounter you, especially if they initiated the break-up, summon all your strength to say that you understand they wanted to end the relationship, and it will take you some time to work that through. Therefore, you would appreciate that they give you the time and space to allow that to happen. That's it. Stop the text. Hang up the phone. Close the door. Walk away.

It may seem unduly harsh, but you are in no emotional state to hold your own at this point with the person who just broke your heart. It will hurt deeply to insist on this complete break, but it is the fastest way to start to heal.

Ideally, in the years to come you may be friends again. But right now you aren't ready for that yet. You haven't changed their status mentally or emotionally, and any communication between the two of you will just prolong the agony. So stop it now until you are over him or her, and then re-examine it.

If you run into them, a simple nod or a hello and a rapid moving along is all you can allow yourself.

RECOVERY PRACTICE # 5 – NO "OLD TIMES' SAKE" DATES

In circumstances where you are in class together or you work together, the chance that you and your ex will partner in some other capacity arises. You may have to do a work project together, and out of the professionalism you will show comes an invitation just to grab lunch "for old times' sake."

You are like a drug addict who has been clean for 20 days and who has just been offered a toke, or an alcohol addict who survived all August without a cold beer and is offered one on a September weekend. Just say no. You are not strong enough to be exposed to your addiction again.

You were a love addict and your ex will deftly take you right back to square one and leave you all confused and feeling even worse than when you broke up the first time.

When recovering from a bad break-up, keep thinking out of sight out of mind. Do not be lured into any circumstances that leave you alone again in any kind of a situation that could even look like or hint at being a date.

If you don't think you are strong enough to say no because you are still desperately attracted to your ex, bite into your reality pill by remembering why you broke up in the first place. That will make it a lot easier.

The danger as you start to recover is that you start to forget the end and keep dwelling fondly on all the good times. But if your ex cheated on you, remember that you deserve someone new in your life who treats you better. You aren't going to find that person when you are wasting your precious time with your ex.

If you just drifted apart and your ex told you they weren't into you anymore, why do you want to invest any effort whatsoever in helping them pass the time? Let them feel alone, because that's sure how you have been feeling!

Under no circumstances should you ever tell your ex that you still love them, even if you feel in your heart that it is true. What you are feeling is loss and grief and even loneliness. That is not love. You had love and it is gone and that's the end of it.

Do not make any effort to contact them for any reason whatsoever. For example, you may know that your ex's mother was having an operation and if you were still together, your inclination would be to call immediately to check on how she is.

As pure as your motives may be (and both you and I know they aren't pure at all), your ex will see right through this and know that you are needy and desperate to have them back. That's the way exes think. It makes them even more powerful and it shows you to be even weaker. It cements for them that they were right in leaving you and it just makes you feel worse.

RECOVERY PRACTICE # 6 – NO STALKING

Love is when we learn how absolutely human we are. Breaking up is when we learn how many different sides humans have.

It is part of our nature that when we are dumped we have an intense curiosity about what our ex is doing without us. Have they started dating someone else? Where are they going, what are they doing? Are they missing you and regretting their decision to go?

At this point, even though you likely don't need to be reminded, we advise you of the "no stalking" rule about getting over a bad break-up.

We know that you can't help but listen when friends come and tell you what your ex is doing, who they are dating, what they are saying and every other tidbit of information they can gather. You may even be tempted to do some spying yourself. You aren't even sure what you are looking for. Perhaps it is just some validation that the person misses you and made a mistake.

That's not going to happen. And as long as you encourage your friends to bring you reports, your healing will be stalled.

The day you are strong enough to say that you don't want to talk about him or her anymore and that you are no longer interested in their activities is the day you take a major step to getting over them.

You just don't need to know those things. There is absolutely nothing people can tell you about them that will make you feel better, and most of it will make you feel a lot worse.

You will look like the unbalanced ex lurking in the background if you keep up such behavior. If they are cruel by nature, they will get devious satisfaction in how they have hurt you. If they are just wanting to move on, you will fall further in their estimation of you. This is a no-win game.

RECOVERY PRACTICE # 7 – THIS MEANS NO FACEBOOK STALKING TOO

Checking on their activities through social media is just as unworthy of you as stalking your ex in person. Promise yourself from day one that you will find the courage to unfriend them from your Facebook account and never look at their pages again.

If you see them having fun and not missing you at all, you will feel lower than low. There is no good that can come of this, not for you and not for them.

RECOVERY PRACTICE # 8 – DON'T ASK THEM TO RECONSIDER

You hurt more than you have ever hurt in your life and we get that. The pain can cloud your rational decision making. But somewhere, deep within that well of strength that has gotten you this far in your young life, you must find the courage to never, ever call your ex and ask them to reconsider taking you back.

If you think for one minute that you can't possibly feel any worse than you do right now, you can. You will feel worse after you have such a conversation.

They will say no. It's over. Not only is the relationship over, it is blown into the dust of time as if it never existed. You cannot change that reality.

At least save your dignity and don't dare make that phone call!

RECOVERY PRACTICE # 9 – IGNORE THEIR NEW LOVE INTEREST

This is the last "don't." Everything in the coming chapters will be on how you can rebuild, but we have to cover this territory because it is so important to your recovery.

The last don't is to avoid trying to learn more information about a new relationship your ex is pursuing. If you run into them, don't ask about the new love interest. Most importantly, never ask what the new person has that you don't. Save your dignity. You won't like the answer anyhow.

Don't compare yourself physically, mentally or intellectually with your successor in your ex's life.

The flip side of this is not to brag about your new love interest to your ex. It's just done. You both deserve to move on and these comparisons have no useful conclusions.

CHAPTER 6

BEGIN TO BUILD A NEW FUTURE FOR YOURSELF

"One's first love is always perfect until one meets one's second love."
– Elizabeth Aston, The Exploits & Adventures of Miss Alethea Darcy

Somewhere in the dark days that follow the end of your relationship and the suffering of the break-up comes a glimmer of light. Sometimes it's in the eyes of a person who looks at you with genuine interest and admiration.

Sometimes it's in a project you get involved in, or a new extra-curricular passion you start to explore.

Or maybe you travel somewhere new and start to envision that the world out there might offer even more adventures than the life story you had been writing.

That is the beginning of recovery, and there are things you can do in this stage to hasten it and make it complete.

The main thing, as mentioned earlier, is to continue to take one single action every day that moves you in the direction of healing and putting your life back together again.

RECOVERY PRACTICE # 10 – IT'S TIME TO STOP TELLING YOUR STORY

The story of your break-up has dominated your life for some time now and everyone around you has been pretty understanding. But lots of other things are happening and nobody has a very concentrated attention span.

Other human tragedies and triumphs supplant you as the hot news item of the week, and friends are starting to change the subject when you go back to the subject of your ex or your grief.

It's time to stop telling your old story and create a new one. Resolve on this day at this time that you aren't going to tell that story again for a solid year, and then only if you see it has any relevance.

To do that, you have to tell other stories and to consider what they will be. Plan your day of change by considering some other topics to chat about. It could be a television show that everyone is watching, an event at your school that you want to get involved in, a workplace activity that sounds like fun, or something that is happening in the life of your friends.

Ask open-ended questions of your friends to encourage them to talk more on this day so you won't have to. Phrase your questions so they start with "what do you think of …." or "how do you feel about…" and add any subject of your choice and then listen. You can effectively steer any conversation this way.

The first day that you go through an entire day without talking about your days in love and out of love will be another good day in your life. You are starting to move on.

RECOVERY PRACTICE # 11 – START TO ENVISION A NEW TOMORROW

At one point, you thought you had your life planned, but now it's time to plan another. You may think you're not ready to do that, but where's the harm in getting started? What do you want to do as a career? Where do you want to study? How do you want to live?

What makes you happy? What kind of work seems like play?

Jot down a few goals. You can change them. Just try them out and see how they feel.

Share some of these ideas with your friends and check out their reactions. Try to consciously align yourself with other friends who have dreams and goals and are getting ready to move enthusiastically into their future.

Open your mind and heart to cultivating some new friendships of both sexes in other parts of your life. If most of your old friends are now "couple friends," branch out to other areas and see who is there. Join a gym, a community group or a church group and get involved in something new. Take up dance or sports or hiking.

RECOVERY PRACTICE # 12 – CREATE A NEW ROUTINE FOR YOURSELF

When you were with your ex, you had little routines built into your life that you cherished and you still miss. As you work your way back from your break-up, begin to create new routines.

Perhaps you balance yourself internally and externally with yoga each morning. Maybe you do a run each night after school or take up a new part-time job that you enjoy.

In particular, look for activities that you and your ex never shared. Order pizza on Friday night but change the toppings to ones you prefer, not the ones your ex always wanted. Go to chick flicks or action movies or anything your ex wouldn't be caught dead at.

Change your hairstyle. Buy a new article of clothing. Move outside of your normal comfort zone.

As you make these changes, you may have a sudden thought that if you change too much, your ex will never come back again. That is a limiting thought that you have to work through and eliminate. Be aware that your ex is likely not thinking about you, so don't waste your time thinking about them. Use the energy you got from being loved to expand your horizons and know that you will someday love again.

Don't be afraid to fill up your life. Later, when you are healed, you will drop some of the activities and enjoy the calmness of your downtime, but right now your goal is to re-engage with the world.

RECOVERY PRACTICE # 13 – TACKLE A NEW EXERCISE PROGRAM

There are two practical reasons for taking up a new exercise routine when recovering from a break-up. The first is that vigorous exercise releases happy hormones in your brain, and despite yourself you feel good again.

The second reason is that going to gyms and taking fitness classes is a great way to meet other people who have happy and healthy outlooks on life, and the enthusiasm is contagious.

It also contributes to your effort to create a new routine for yourself. Knowing you have a Zumba class every Tuesday or community soccer games on Thursday takes away the endless days of "what will I do now that my love has gone?" At least a couple of long evenings have been filled.

You may feel more inclined to take long, lonely walks at this point, but force yourself to opt for the group activity. It will pull you out of your pain faster. The conversation you hear in group activities centers on different topics from what you might normally discuss and will stimulate your thinking as well as exercise your body.

RECOVERY PRACTICE # 14 – MAKE NEW FRIENDS, NOT LOVERS

You do need new people in your life. You don't need a new lover, at least not yet.

Any way that you package it, a rebound relationship is a bad idea.

Rather than making your ex jealous or helping you move on, jumping into a new intense relationship will actually just make your ex shrug their shoulders in indifference and make you stall your recovery.

The problem is you never really love the rebound boyfriend or girlfriend. You just transfer the feelings you felt for your ex onto them and hope that they will turn into your ex. They won't.

You aren't being fair to yourself or to the other person with whom you get involved. You might end up treating them just as badly as you have been treated yourself. That will just compound your bad feelings about yourself.

CHAPTER 7

THE THREE FOUNDATIONS OF A RENEWED AND HAPPY LIFE

"Something about first love defies duplication. Before it, your heart is blank. Unwritten. After, the walls are left inscribed and graffitied. When it ends, no amount of scrubbing will purge the scrawled oaths and sketched images, but sooner or later, you find that there's space for someone else, between the words and the margins."

– Tammara Webber, Where You Are

*W*e are told so often that time heals all wounds that we start to think of it as a cliché. That may be, but it is also true.

There is no defined time period for how long it takes to wake up some morning, go through an entire day, and fall asleep that night without once thinking about your ex, but after a period of time, unless you seriously jeopardize yourself, it inevitably happens.

It is important as you rebuild your life that you realize time is on your side and you do not have to adhere to some mysterious, dictated schedule.

Instead, you just have to get up every day and take one step towards healing, and you will get there.

RECOVERY PRACTICE # 15 – PUT OFF MAJOR DECISIONS FOR A MONTH

When long-time spouses are separated by the death of the other, the standard advice is to avoid making any major decisions for one year.

When you are recovering from a relationship, faster recoveries are anticipated and the general rule is to avoid making big life changes for one to three months.

Just as you need to avoid rebound relationships, you also want to avoid rebound decisions.

After one month, if you still want to enter a convent or become a monk, or you want to backpack around Europe for a year, you will be in a better position to evaluate the wisdom of your decision. If you do it spontaneously, you are simply running and your problems and heartache just run with you.

If you feel strongly that there is a new road in life you want to travel, mark that idea in your diary for one month from today to be reconsidered. You can reasonably move it ahead a month at a time for three months before you either embrace it or discard it, at least for now.

RECOVERY PRACTICE # 16 – PURSUE A NEW HOBBY

Start piano lessons. Enroll in an art class. Learn to use sign language. Take a first aid course. Go for your lifeguard badge. Learn to cook great Italian food. Go horseback riding.

One of the most creative things you can do to heal is begin to shift that time you spend hurting into time spent learning something new and intriguing to you. Think about something you would really like to pursue and get started.

There will never be a better time.

RECOVERY PRACTICE # 17 – MAKE SURE YOU SLEEP ENOUGH

Whether you are recovering from a physical or mental illness, sleep is a balm that sooths and nudges us back to health.

When you are seriously upset about things, like your break-up, it is not unusual to find your sleep disrupted. You crawl into bed, exhausted from your stressful day and longing for the relief that sleep brings, but your brain just can't seem to shut down.

You start to think of all the negative thoughts you have been dealing with, and all of a sudden it's three o'clock in the morning and you are still tossing and turning.

Promise yourself that you are allowed to think those thoughts earlier in the evening if you need to work them through. But after 9 p.m., rescind that permission you give yourself to be consumed by your negative thoughts.

Instead, create a sleep ritual. You may take a hot, aromatherapy style bath, drink a cup of hot chocolate and watch a few good shows on Netflix or read a good book. Try to stay off of computer and cell phone and slowly unwind.

When the stress of your heartache threatens your calmness, be strong and close it down. Think about the scent of your bath, the aroma of the hot chocolate or the vision of blue skies and woolly sheep.

Try to sleep unaided by medications as soon as possible after your break-up. It will help you perhaps more than anything else to fuel your come-back.

Since falling asleep is all about learning to be in the moment, you might find it helpful to do mindfulness breathing to relax yourself once you are in bed. Simply focus all your attention on your breath.

Exhale and then inhale as deeply as you can three times, all the while trying to focus on nothing but your breath and the way it feels going in and out of your body. It sounds easy, but it is much more difficult than it sounds. By the third breath, all kinds of other thoughts want to intrude. When that happens, do not be angry with yourself. Just accept that it has happened and refocus your full attention on your breath.

Know that you are not alone with your sleep challenges. In fact, Dr. Avi Sadeh of Tel Aviv University did a controlled study of students' sleep habits and discovered that if they allowed their thoughts to focus on their stress and anxiety, they were less likely to sleep than those who could focus on being in the moment.

He concluded that sleep does have the power to help people regulate their personal tension and stress, particularly in dealing with situations that they had no control over.

Meanwhile, Harvard University's Women's Health Watch reports that lack of sleep can make you irritable, impatient, unable to concentrate and prone to moodiness, none of which are qualities linked to recovery from a bad break-up.

RECOVERY PRACTICE # 18 – ALCOHOL AND DRUGS WON'T HELP

While crying in your beer is the break-up remedy most recommended in country songs over the years, in reality it does little to make the situation any better. And drowning your sorrows in alcoholic beverages or blotting them out with drugs can create serious problems in the long run. Take up herbal tea or a healthy juice blend instead.

If you have used drugs to help you cope and believe that you are developing a problem, please speak with your parents or a trusted adult to get help.

CHAPTER 8

RE-EXAMINE THE RELATIONSHIP

"That's it. Love makes us all strong."
– E.A. Bucchianeri, Brushstrokes of a Gadfly

Bit by bit, as the days pass and you begin to see that the sunshine is still pleasant and the stars still light up the night sky, you begin to look at the world a little differently.

You begin to not be sorry that you have had the experience of intense love and to wonder if it could ever feel like that again.

That is the point when you are ready to re-examine the relationship that has ended.

RECOVERY PRACTICE # 19 – TIME TO LOOK AT YOU LOVER AGAIN

When you feel emotionally stable, allow yourself a designated afternoon or evening to reconsider how you are growing now as a person and examine if you could have continued to develop had you stayed in that relationship.

What parts weren't good? What parts really worked? If you can be honest now, were there things about your ex that always bothered you a little bit but that you learned to overlook?

Were there areas of your relationship that would have inevitably led to conflict had you stayed together? Why did your ex feel that you had grown apart? If you were betrayed by someone you trusted who cheated with your ex, how have you come to terms with that relationship?

Do you think you are more mature now than before your heart was broken? Are you stronger or weaker? Can some good come out of this experience?

Allow time for a reasonable reflection of the events and consider what you have learned about yourself in the process. This is all part of self-development.

RECOVERY PRACTICE # 20 – GO FOR A COMPLETE CHANGE OF ATTITUDE

People who go through life feeling empowered and positive end up building a life beyond what they could imagine.

Jason Connell, who founded the program "Changing the World 101," wrote about why attitude matters in a blog. He says that the secret to overcoming any setback in life is to adopt an attitude that allows you to feel positive and empowered.

Our parents used to call it making lemonade when life handed you a lemon; he calls it asking if you can still solve your problem another way if the first way didn't work.

There are three secrets to being empowered in life, he writes. The first is to avoid people who suck the life right out of you and leave you feeling empty and betrayed (that would be your ex).

The second thing is to focus everything you have on the positive side of situations. One trick how to do this is in any crisis or horrible situation, grab a pen and write down one good thing that can result from it.

The third thing is to stop complaining. Connell is so passionate about that third point that he has actually launched a program called the "Complain Free World Challenge." His theory is that if you can go 21 consecutive days without complaining, great things start to happen. You could always try it and see if he's right.

Balance these changes by adding one more: let go of your negative thoughts. There's an old saying that misery loves company but if it does, it doesn't last long. If you are trying to rebuild yourself, surrounding yourself with friends who have a positive outlook on life is one of the easiest ways to life your own spirits.

Cultivate your positive perspective on life and grow your patience to deal with things that go wrong. Learn to step back from bad things that happen in life and regain your sense of how they fit into your entire world. Most importantly, try not to let any one thing become your entire world.

Just as you wouldn't put all your financial investments into one place for fear if that bank or financial institution folded you would be broke, don't put all your emotional investments into one person. That is not to say you shouldn't love completely, but don't look for the person who completes you. Go into the relationship complete yourself and enjoy the gifts of the relationship as an equal.

RECOVERY PRACTICE # 21 – GET READY TO DATE AGAIN

Getting back into the dating scene can be daunting when you have been living life as part of couple. But there are three actions that you can take to make it easier.

The first is to go ahead and accept the invitations of your friends to meet people, even if they are setting up a blind date for you. They have been given a bad reputation, perhaps well-deserved in some cases but exaggerated in others.

For every blind date that ends in a disappointing and awkward evening there is at least the potential to make a new acquaintance. Discerning friends can have the uncanny knack of playing matchmaker successfully too, so don't rule their efforts out.

The second technique is to push yourself into an activity that attracts other people who may also be single. Join things like hiking groups, sports teams, and volunteer groups. Working together on a team or for a common cause brings people together, and if you're lucky enough you might find even find someone who catches your eye.

Thirdly, make up a list of things that you have always thought would be fun, but never found the time to do. They can be little things like going to an art gallery opening, museum, paintball, bungee jumping, or even taking dance classes. Round out your list with recipes you want to try, skills you want to learn and places you want to visit.

When you hit a lonely patch, go to your idea journal and pick something interesting to do. You often meet very interesting people when you embark on your own adventures.

RECOVERY PRACTICE # 22 - RE-BUILD YOUR SELF-ESTEEM

When you endure a break-up, your self-esteem takes a hit. By that we mean the value we place on ourselves.

To go on and find love again, it is important to know that you are worthy of love and that you are lovable. You have to know that you are unique and a worthwhile person.

How do you manage to portray yourself as all of those things when you meet new people if inside of you there is a little voice reminding you that someone found you unlovable, ordinary, and not worthy of their time?

It is tough to get your esteem back, but there are some techniques that will help.

One way is taking the time to gather knowledge about yourself so that you can better gauge what you will likely do in certain circumstances. Take a pen and paper in hand now and write down five strengths of character that you know you have. Now write five things about yourself that you wish to change.

Do not judge what you have written, just accept who you are. You can work on changing things you like or don't like later; right now, you just need to acquire self-knowledge.

If someone were to introduce you as a guest speaker, what would they say about you? If you won an award in life, what would it be for?

The reason self-knowledge and self-esteem are so vital is because if you do not know yourself and value yourself as a person, it will be virtually impossible for you to fall in love again. You will instead hide behind a wall built to keep out the hurt should a new love go bad, and never find the courage to commit again. That is not a good way to go through life.

Experts at the Mayo Clinic suggest that knowing the situation that eroded your self-esteem is a good first step to re-building it. It is vital that you allow yourself time to contemplate how you interpret what happened to you and whether or not you played a role in what happened.

Whether you did or you didn't doesn't matter as much as you recognizing your role in the break-up. Did you miss messages your ex was trying to send you? Did you really listen for the meaning behind the words spoken?

One technique for really getting to know yourself better is to try asking yourself common questions that you would hear on a job interview or in a dating game situation. Do your honest answers surprise you?

Asking and answering these questions is the only way you can learn and grow from the experience that has happened.

Now broaden your inquiry to the world in general. Do you see the world as a happy place or one on the verge of collapse? If it is the latter, your challenge to become more positive and open to the world will be tough to achieve.

The process of building yourself up after a bad fall is rough at times, but it is also invigorating. You emerge stronger, more spirited and ready for more adventure. You know now that no matter how bad it gets, you can survive it. That is valuable knowledge to carry with you through life.

I want to personally thank all of you who purchased this book.

Can I ask you for a favor?

If you found this book helpful I would really appreciate if you could leave a quick review on Amazon for my book.

I love hearing from my readers and read all of my reviews. Book reviews are SO important for independent authors like me to help get my work out to a larger audience!

Thanks,

Emilee Day

Made in the USA
Middletown, DE
25 May 2023

31475267R00040